THE NATURE OF COLOURING

AN ENGLISH GARDEN

A COLLECTION OF ORIGINAL PHOTOGRAPHS
FROM ENGLISH GARDENS AND COUNTRYSIDE
FOR COLOURING IN

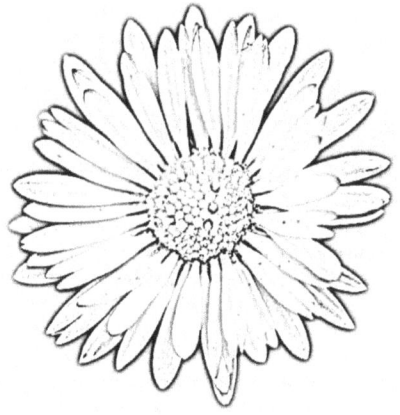

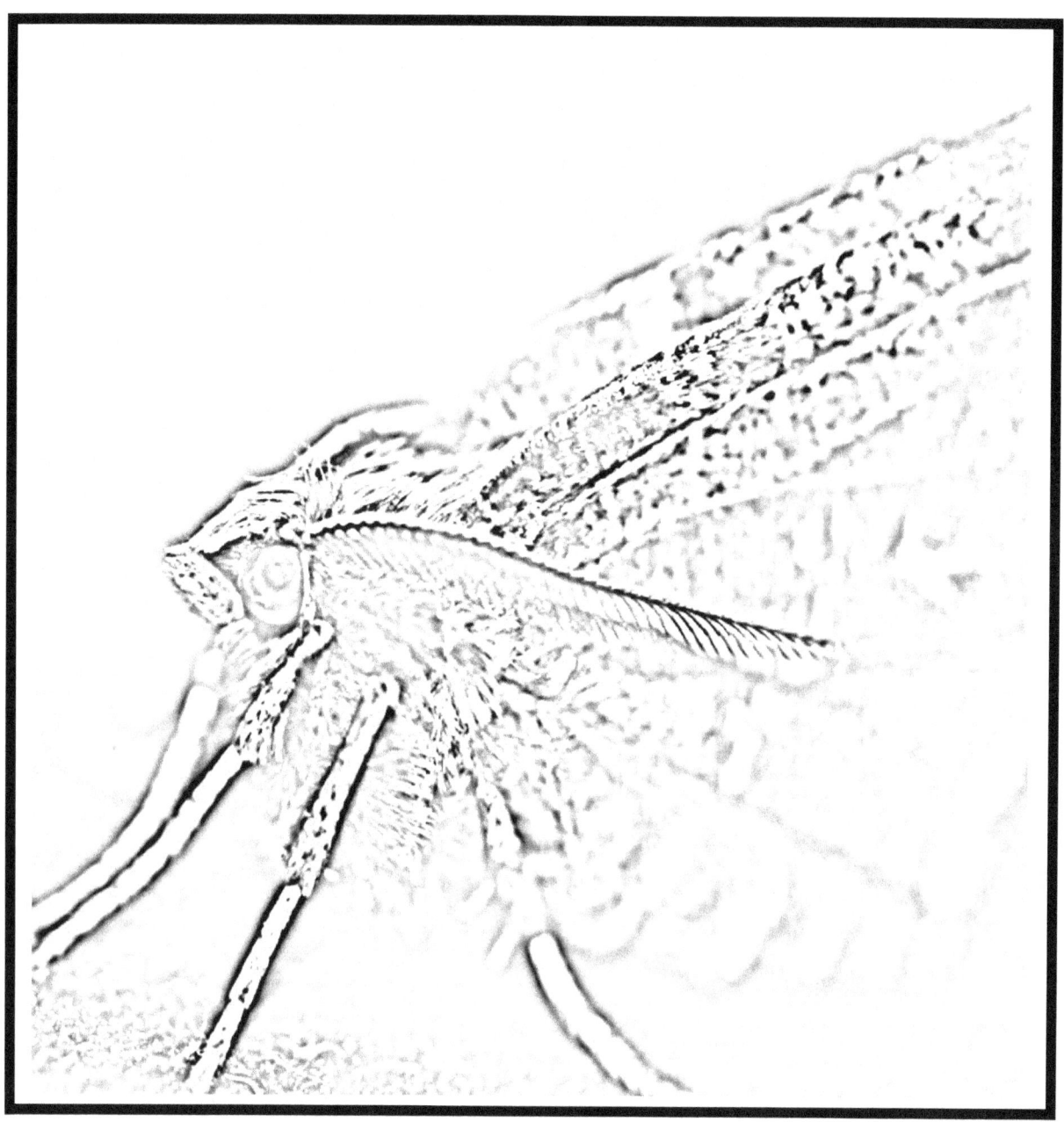

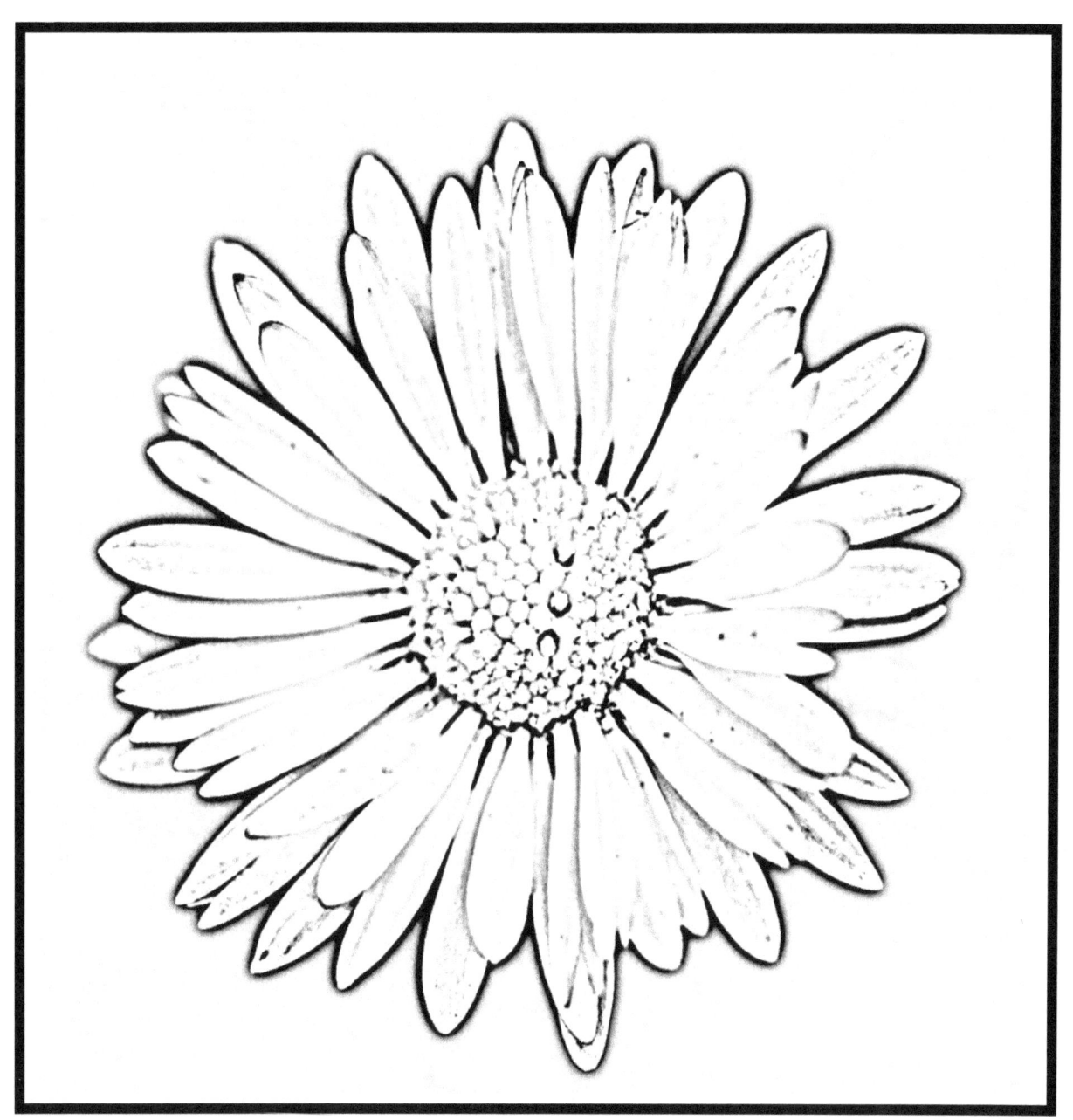

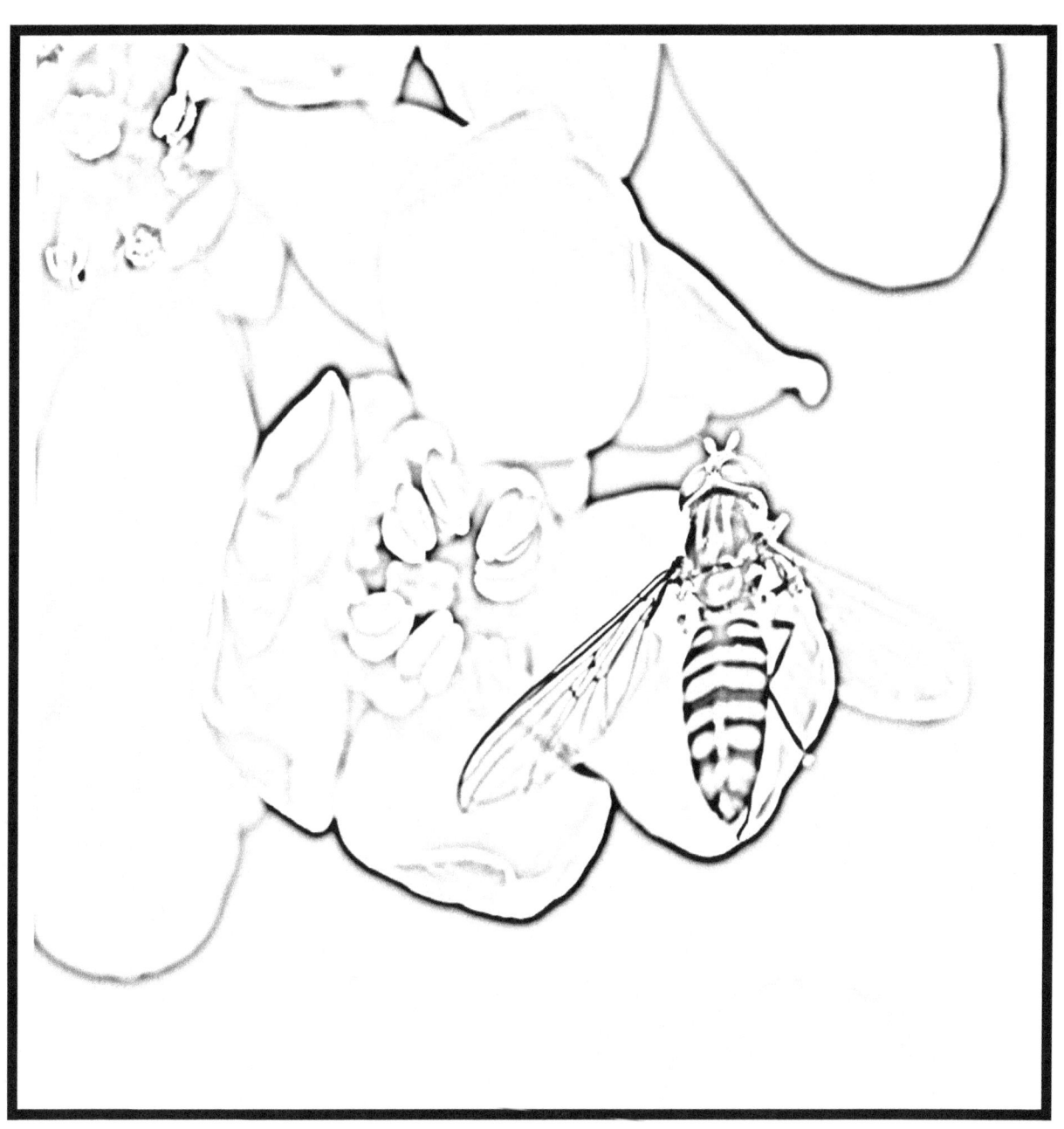

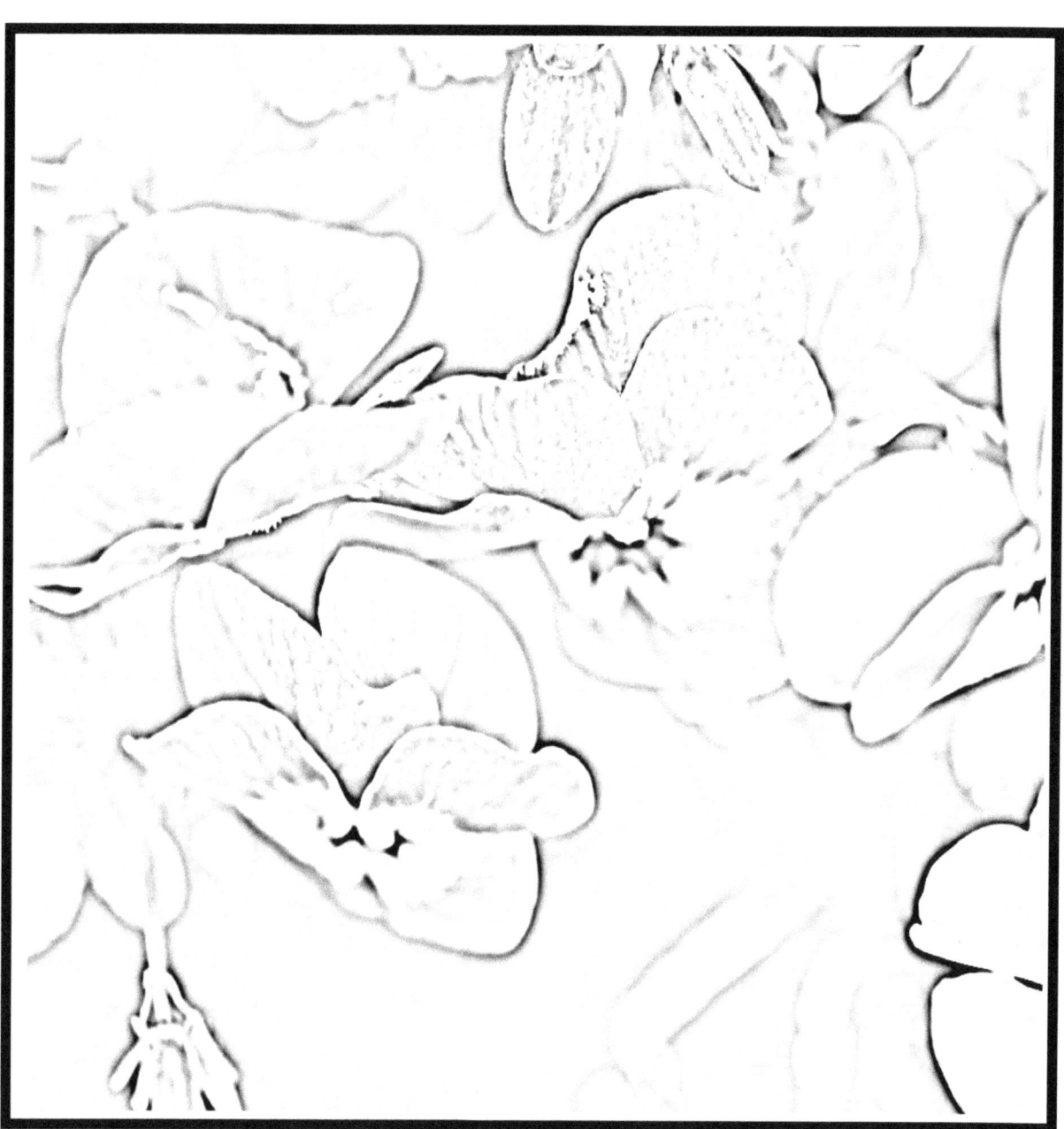

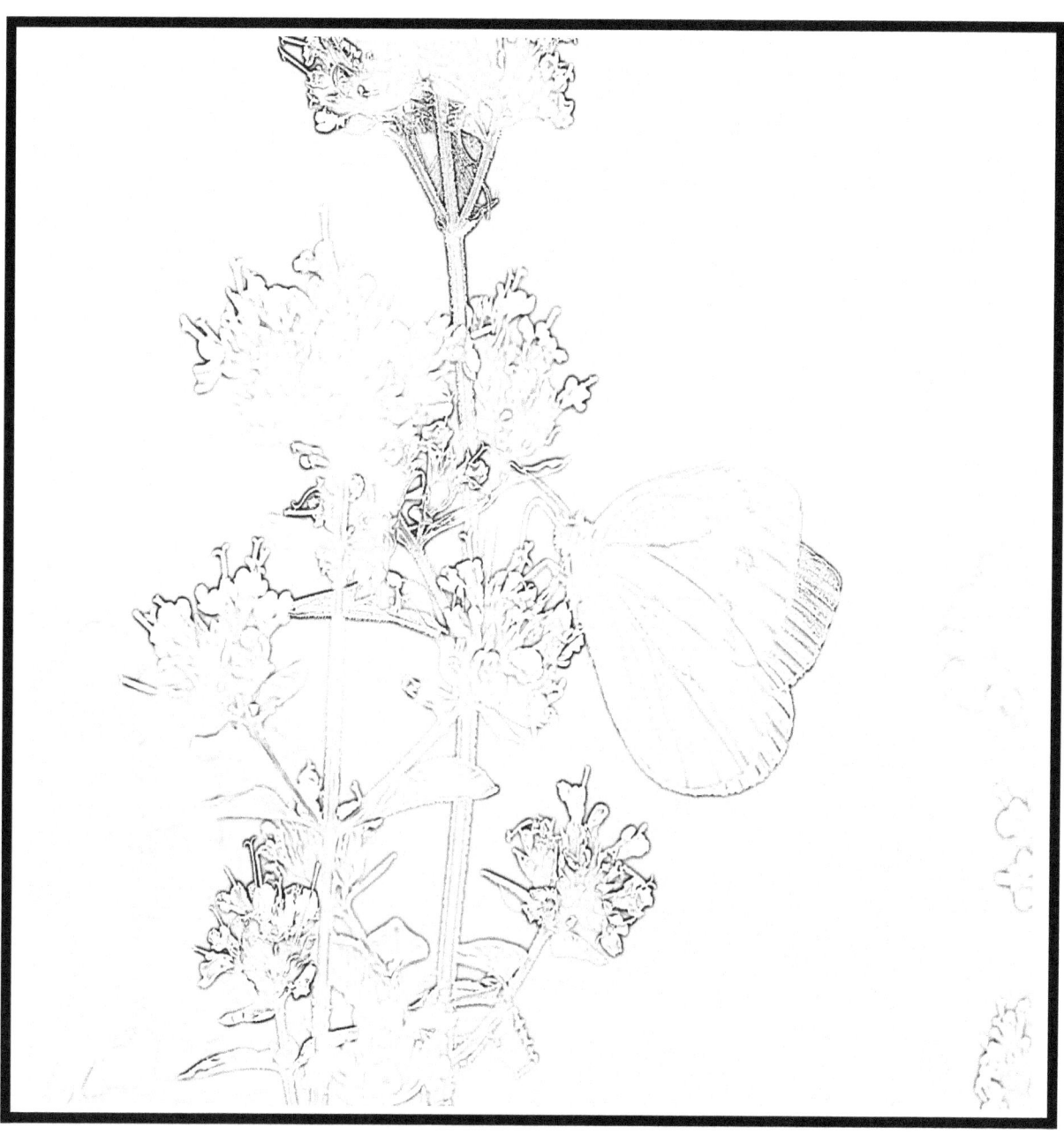

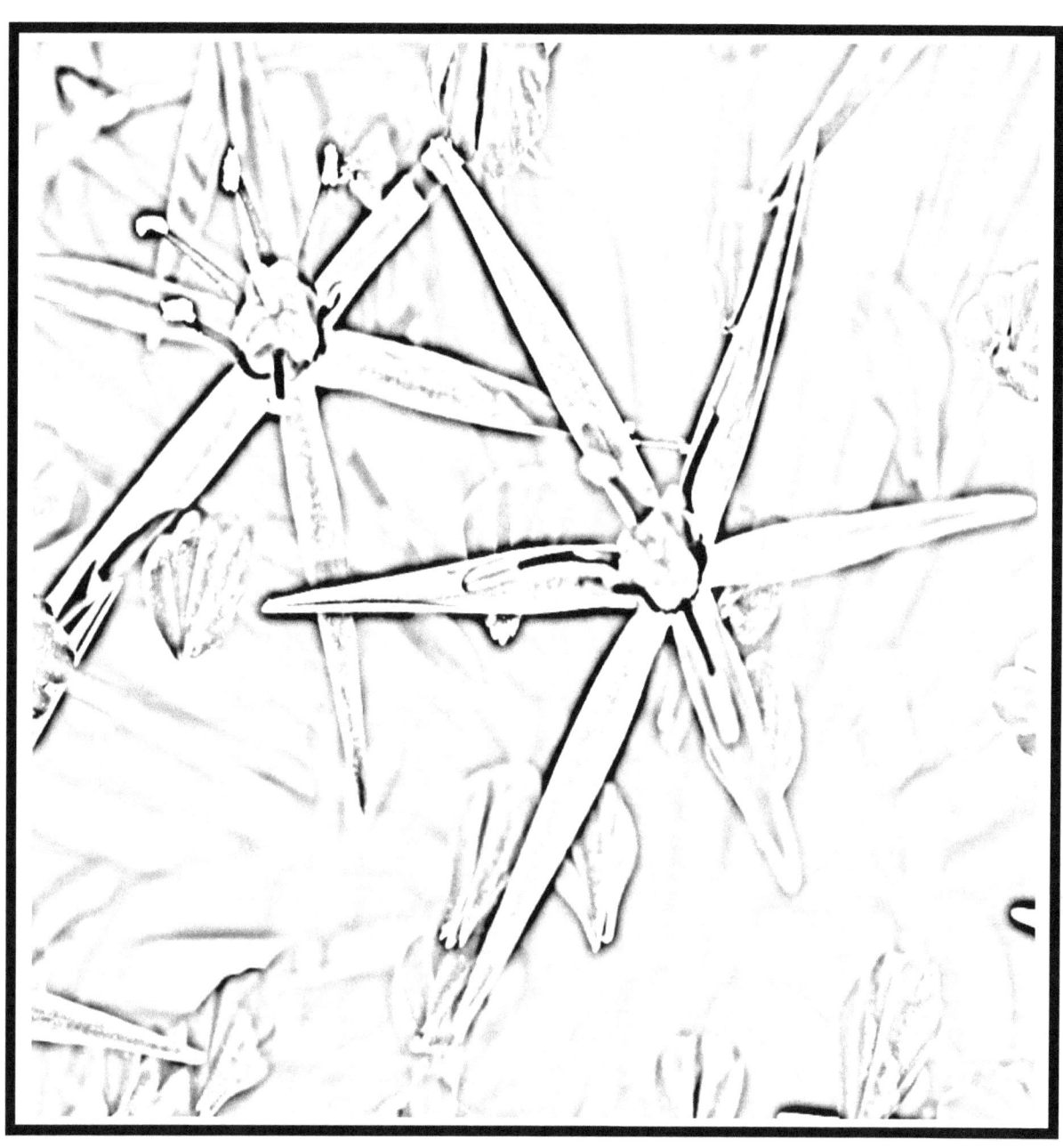

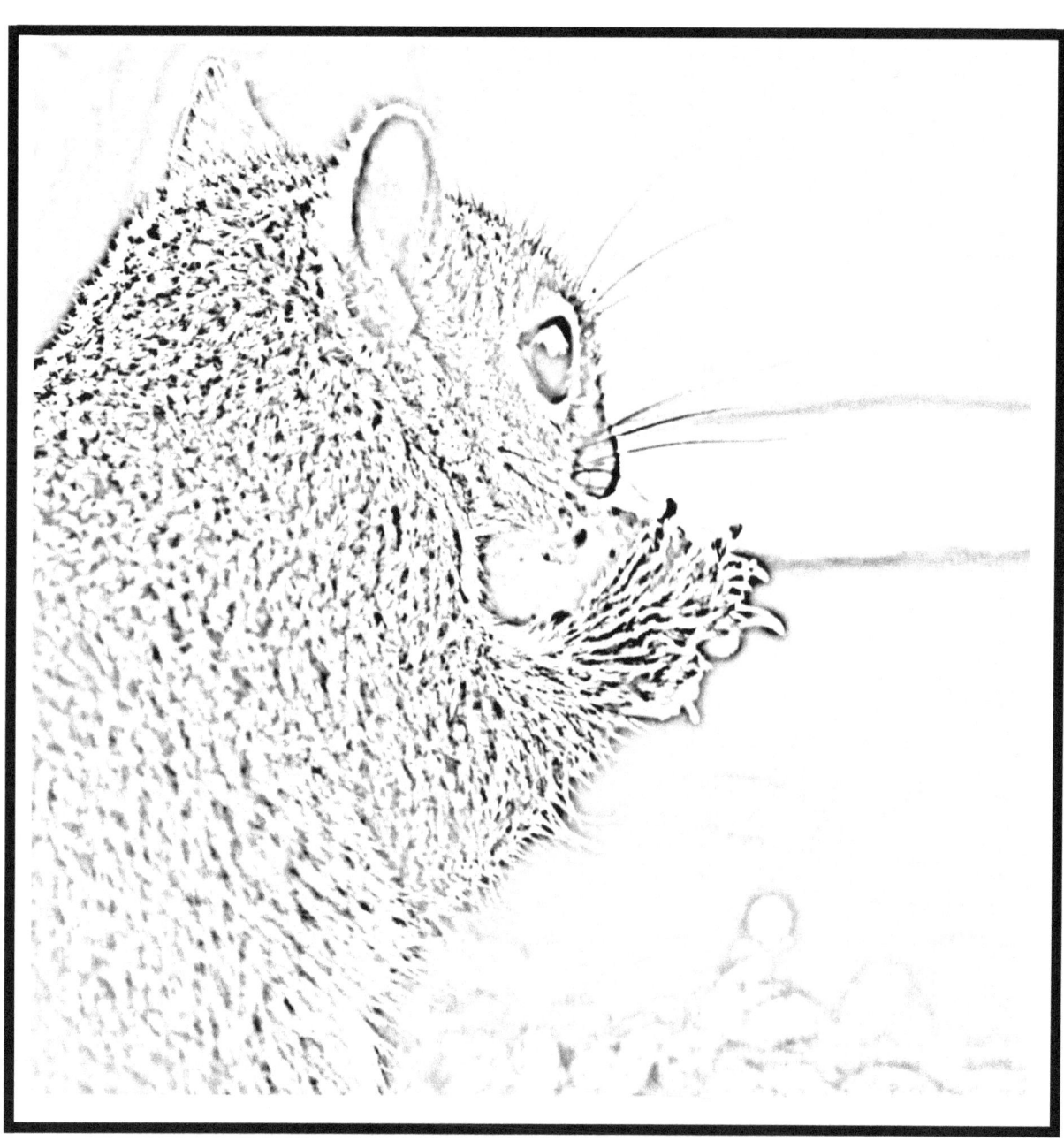

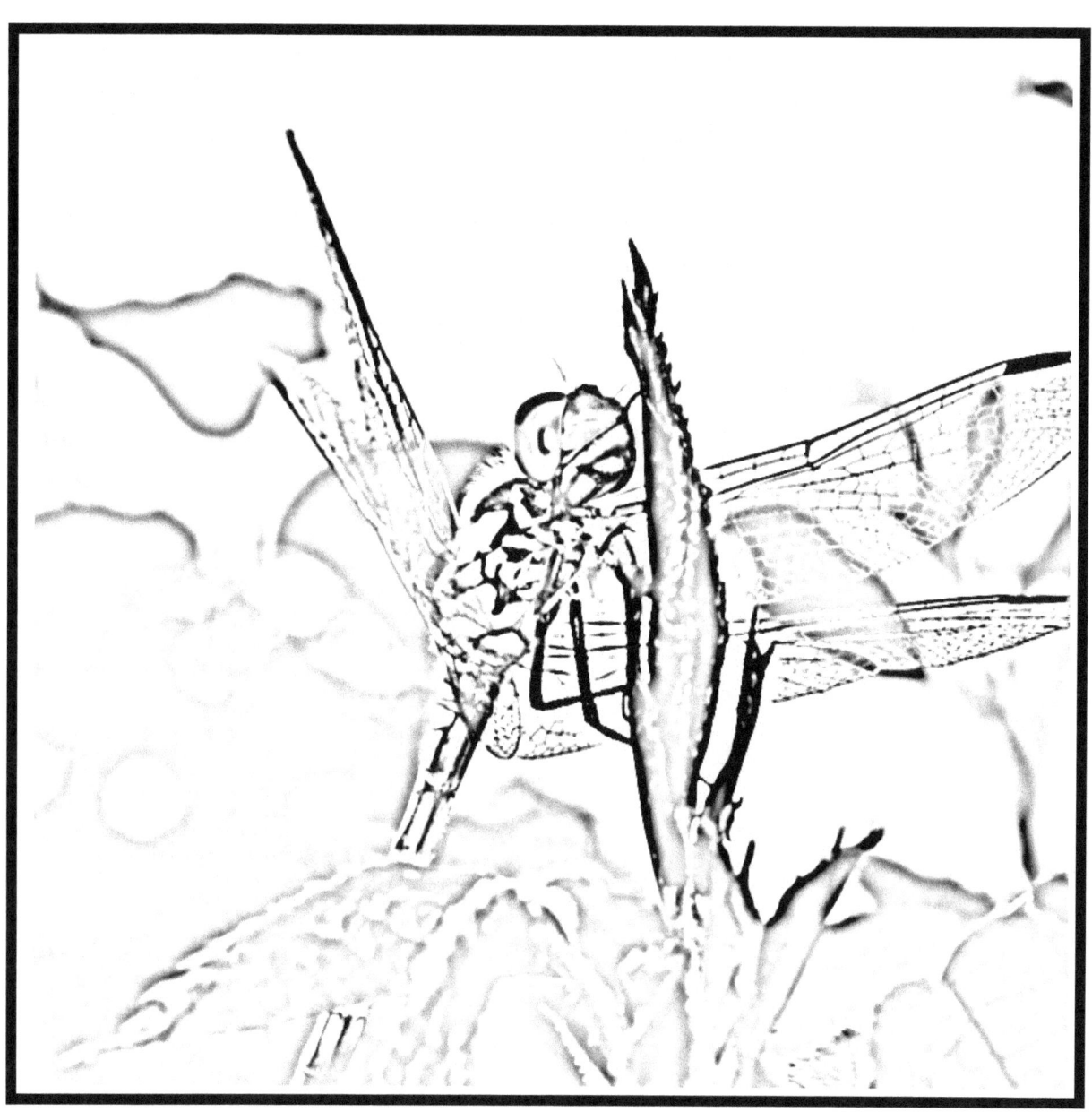

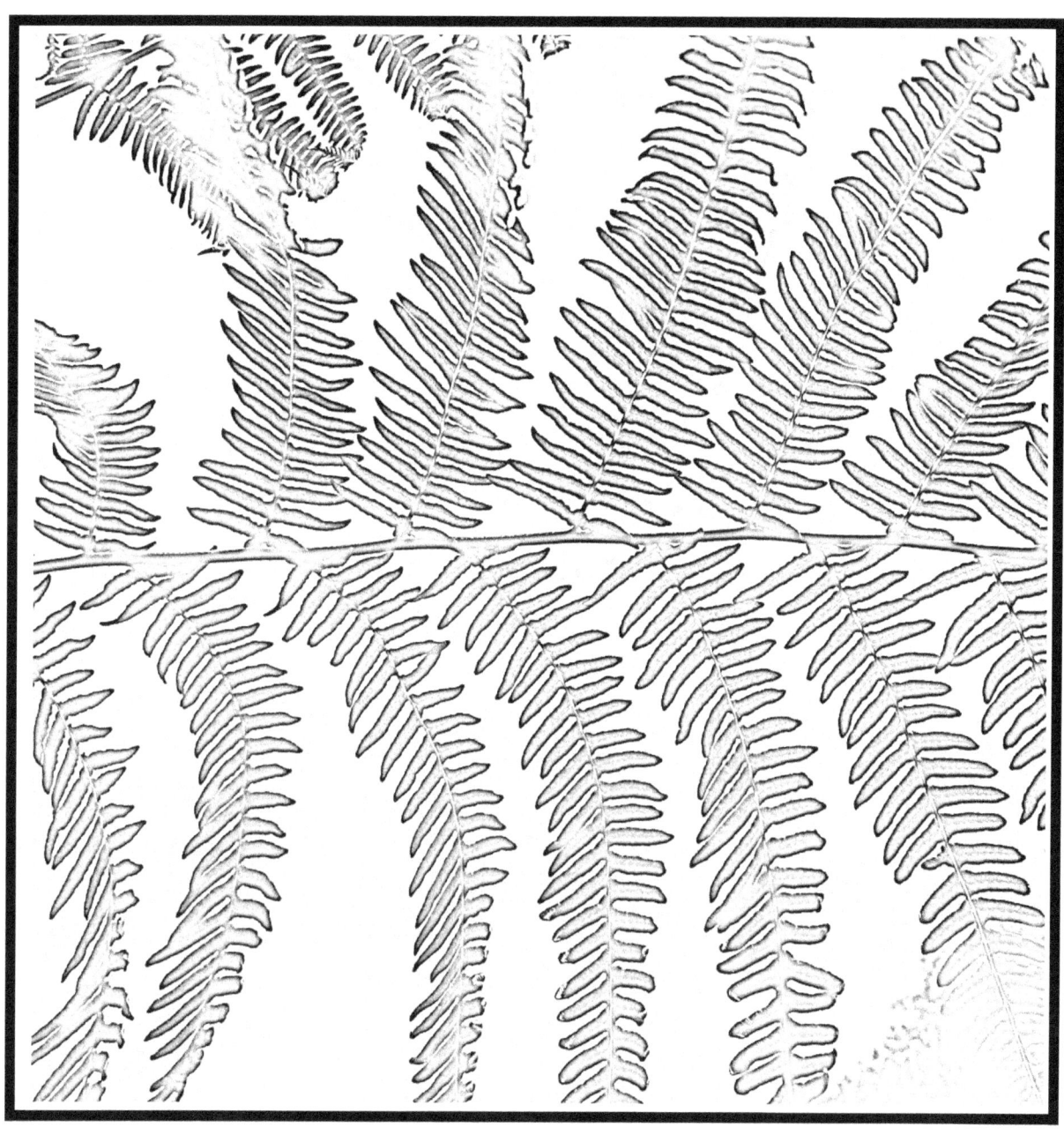

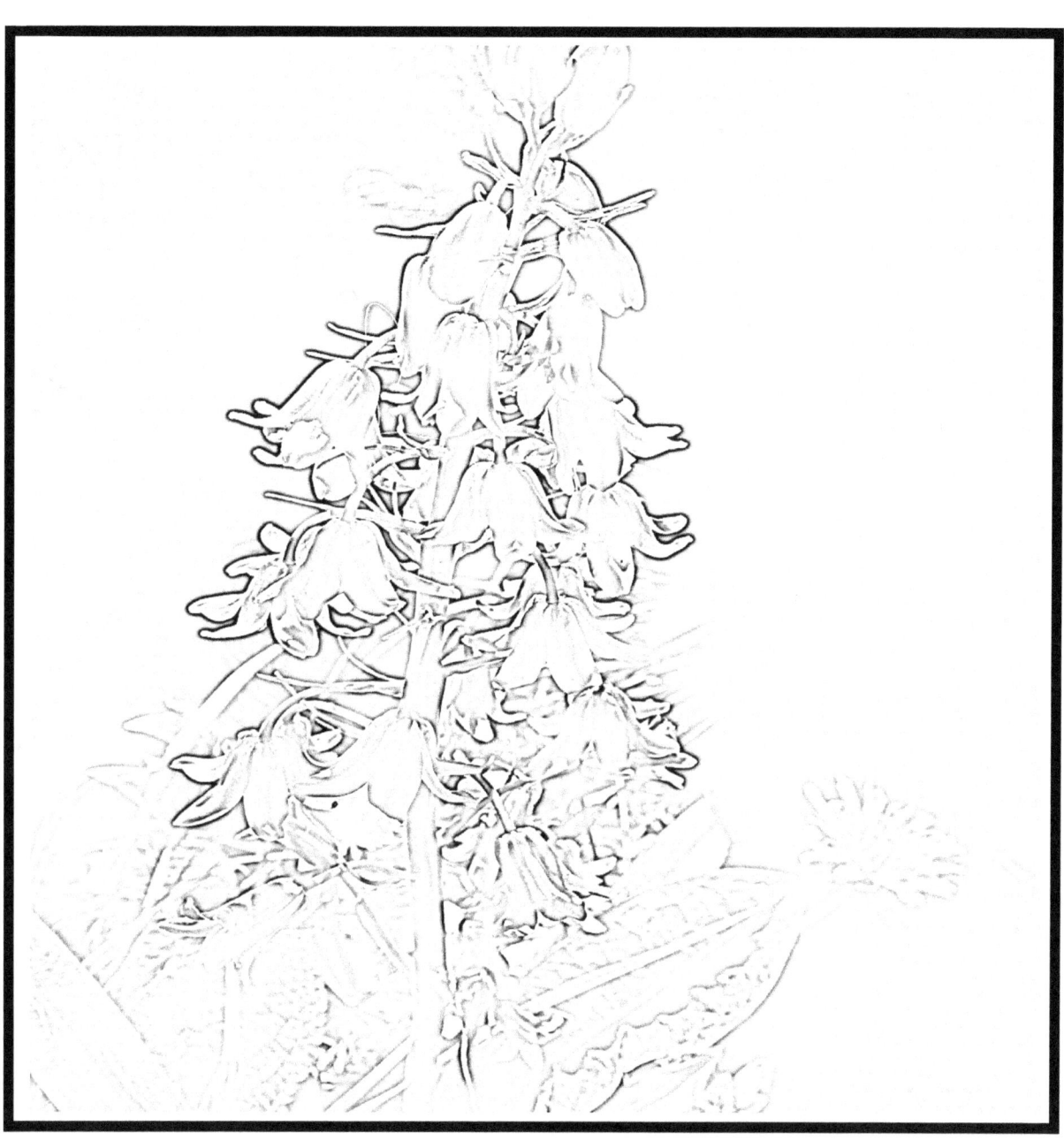

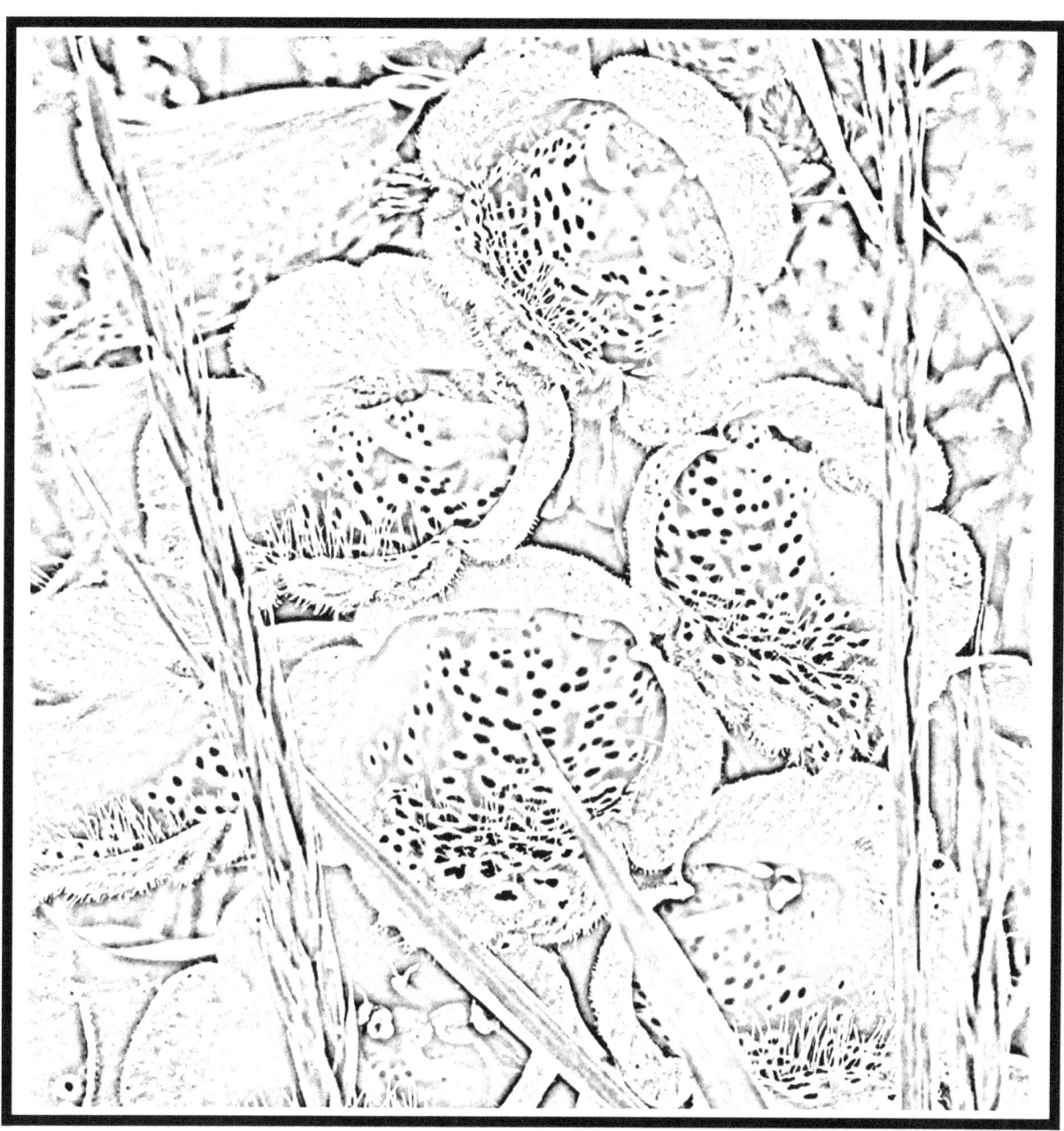

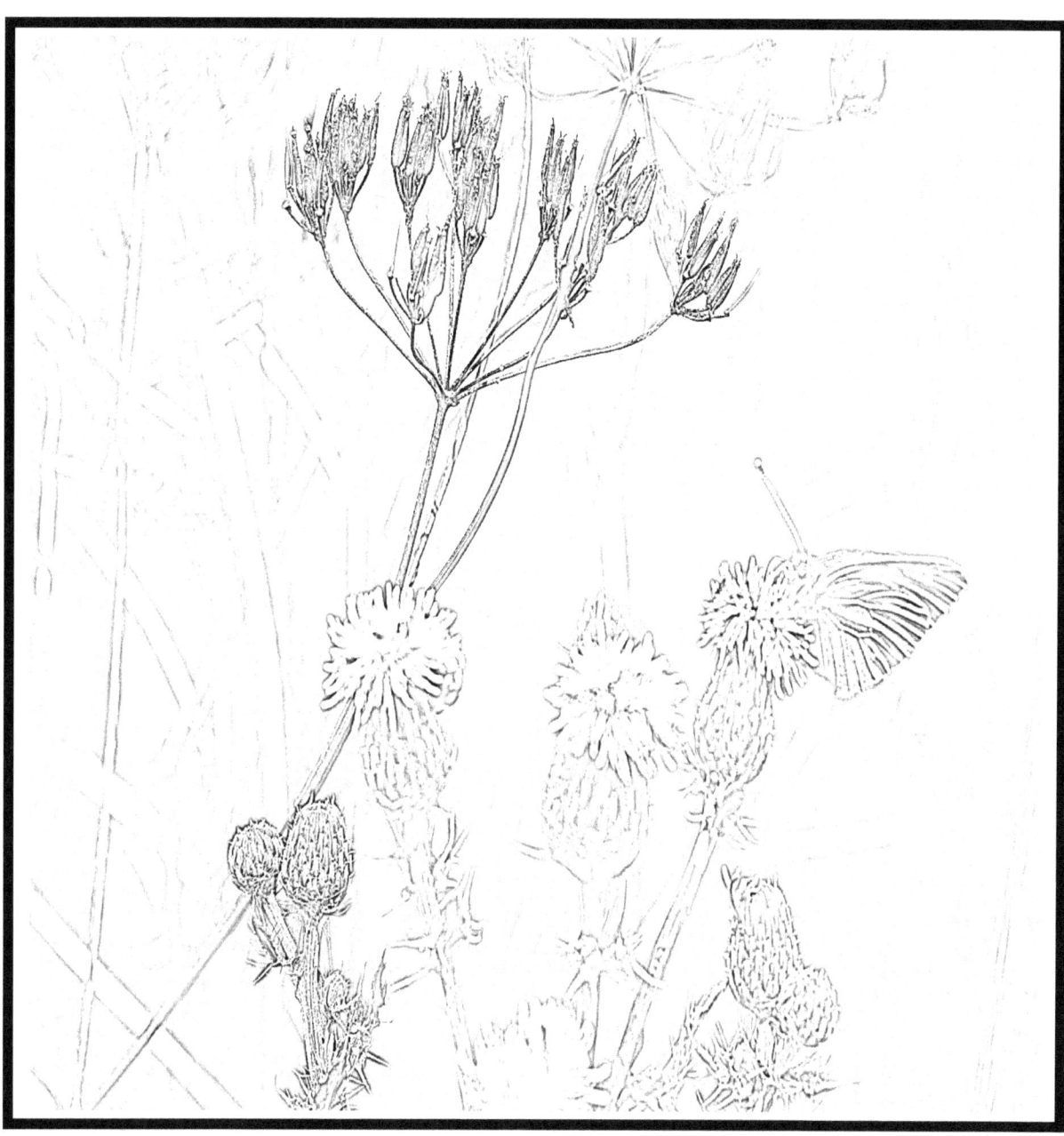

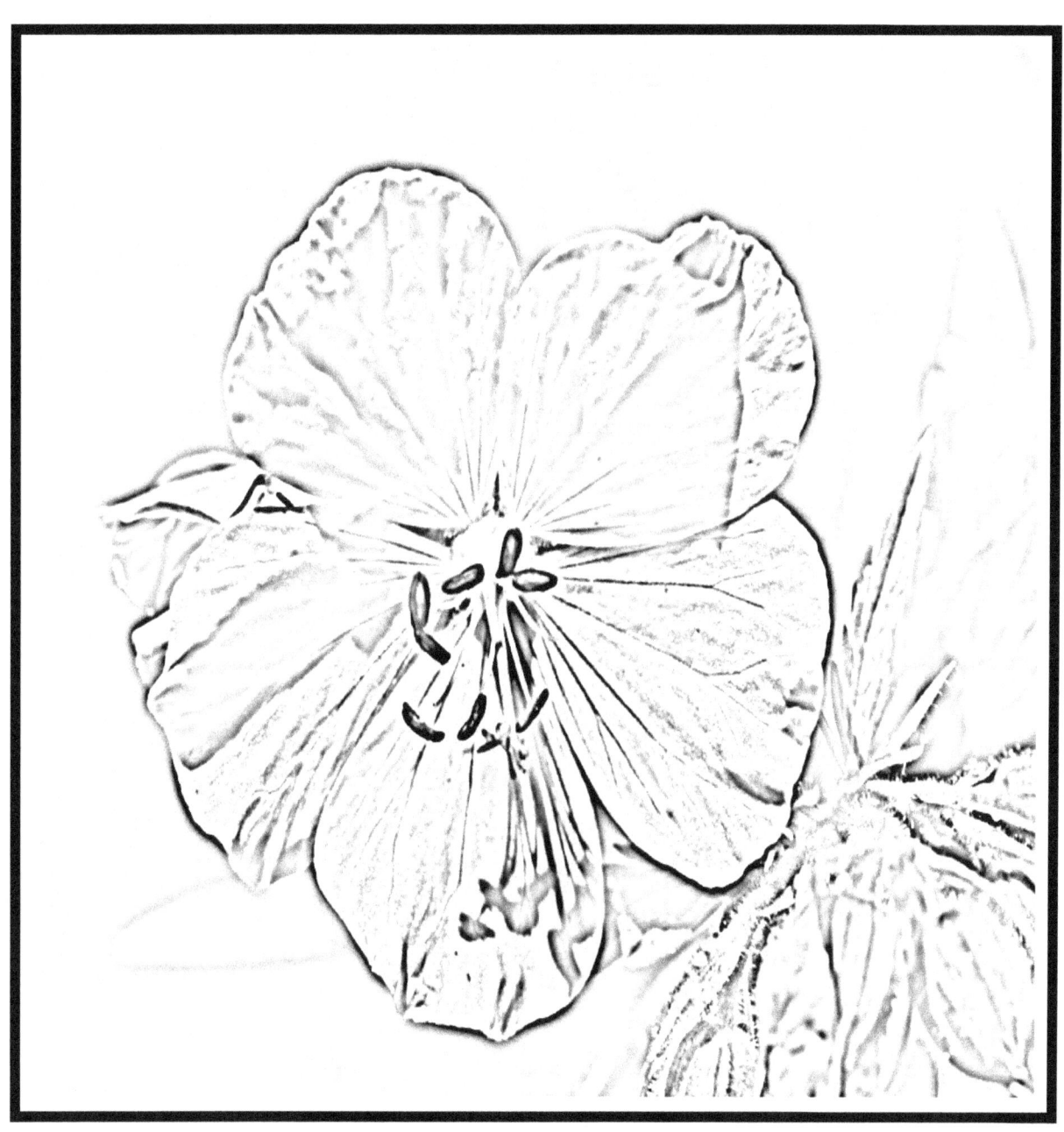

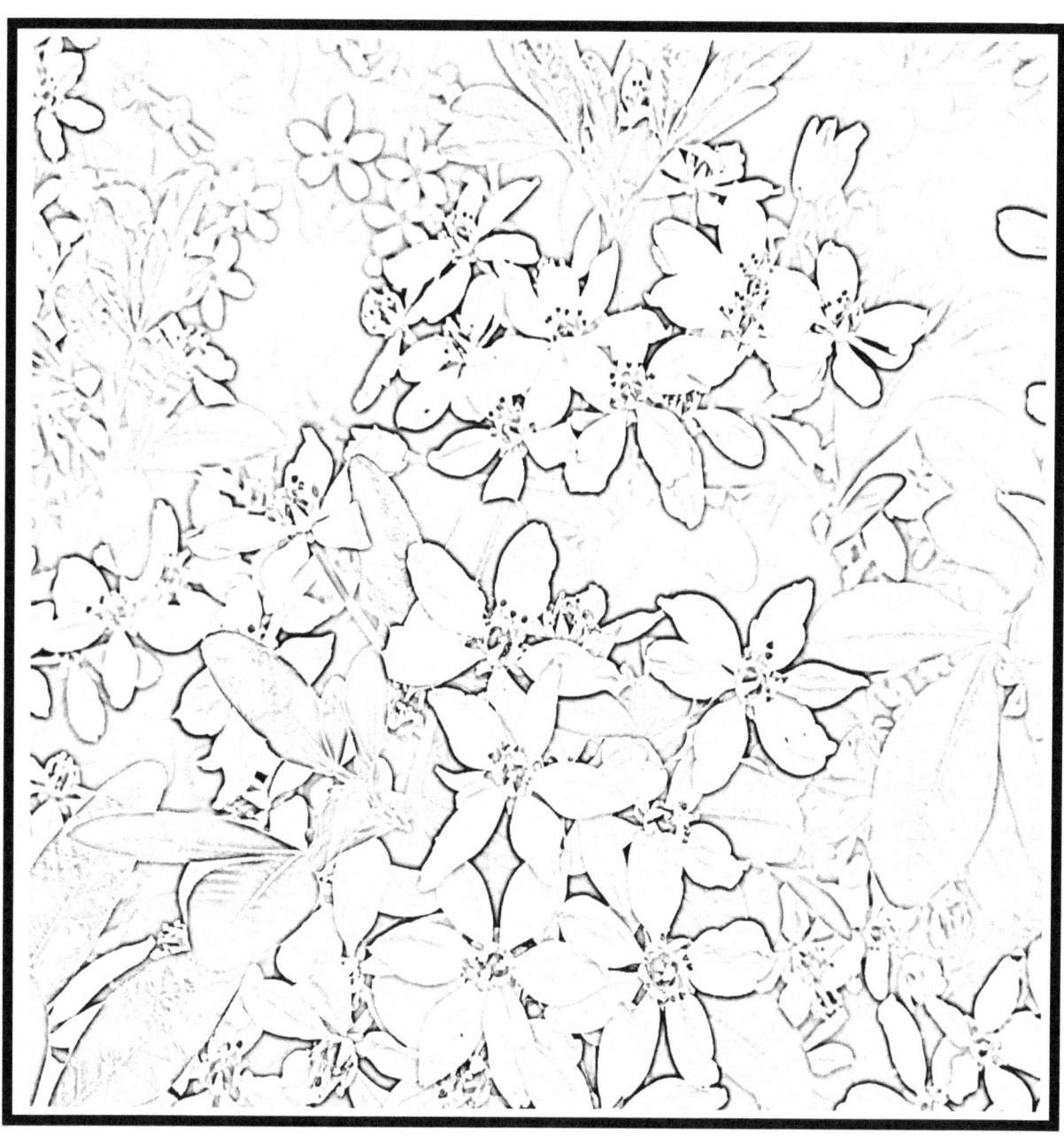

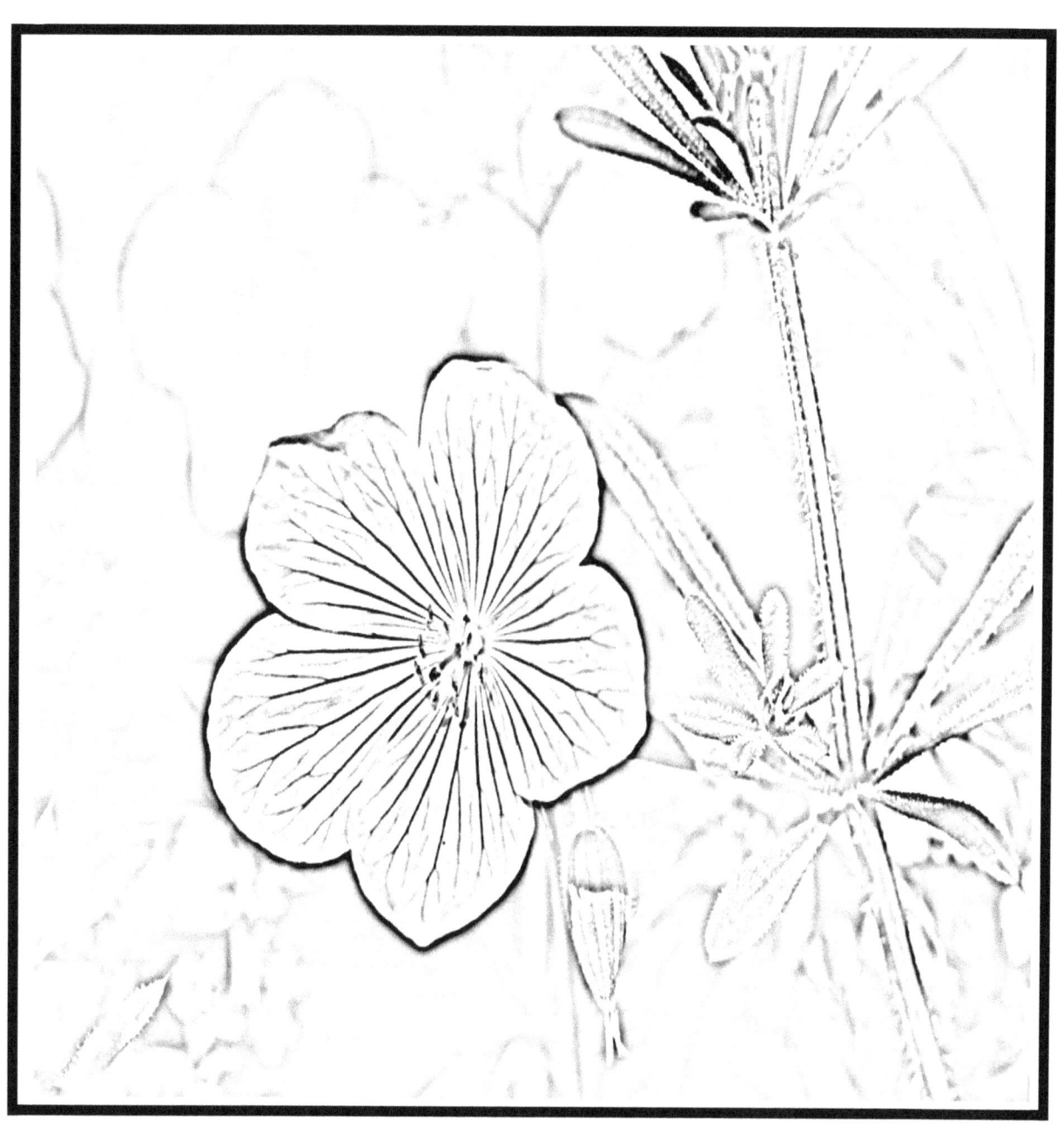

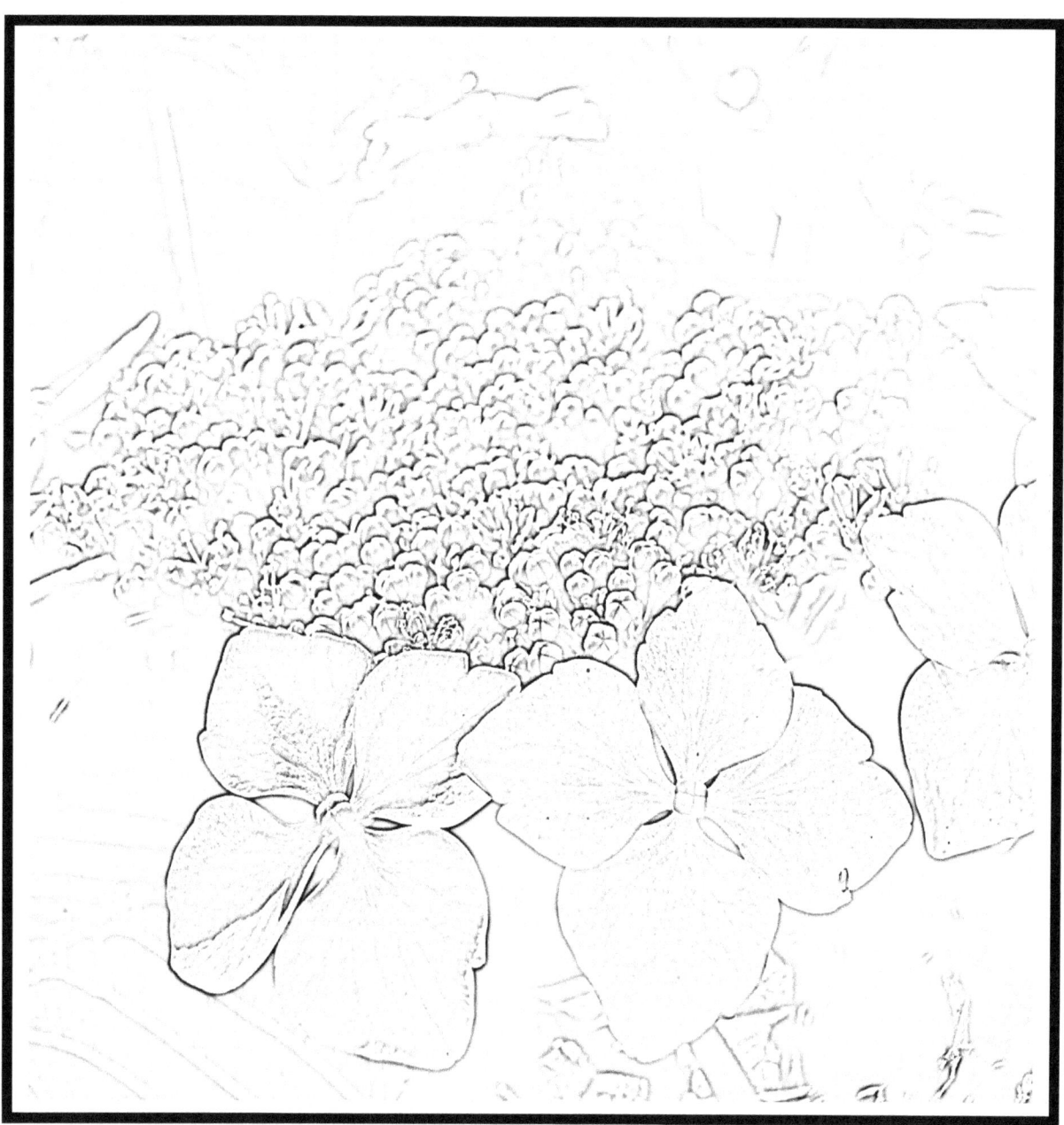

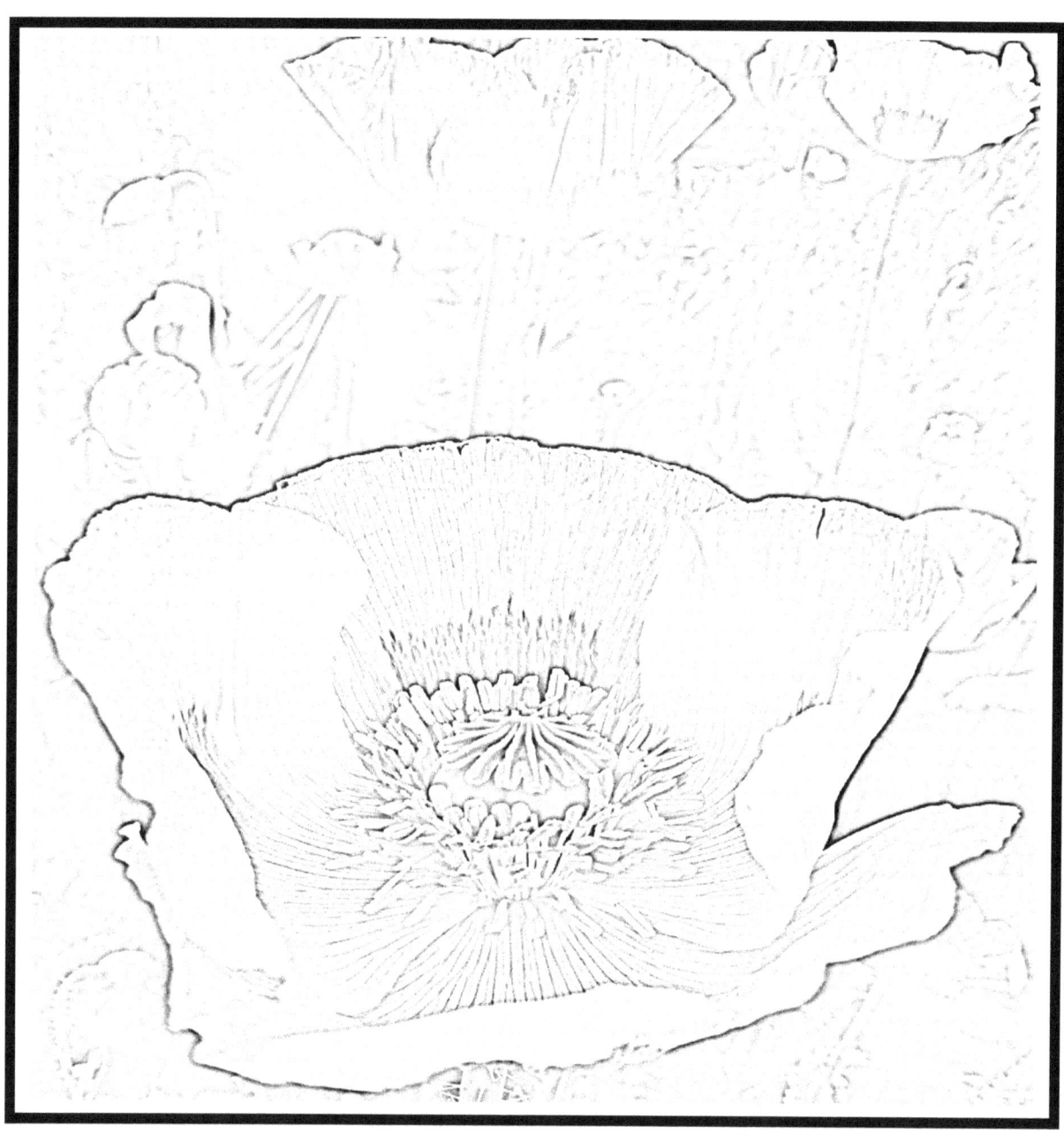

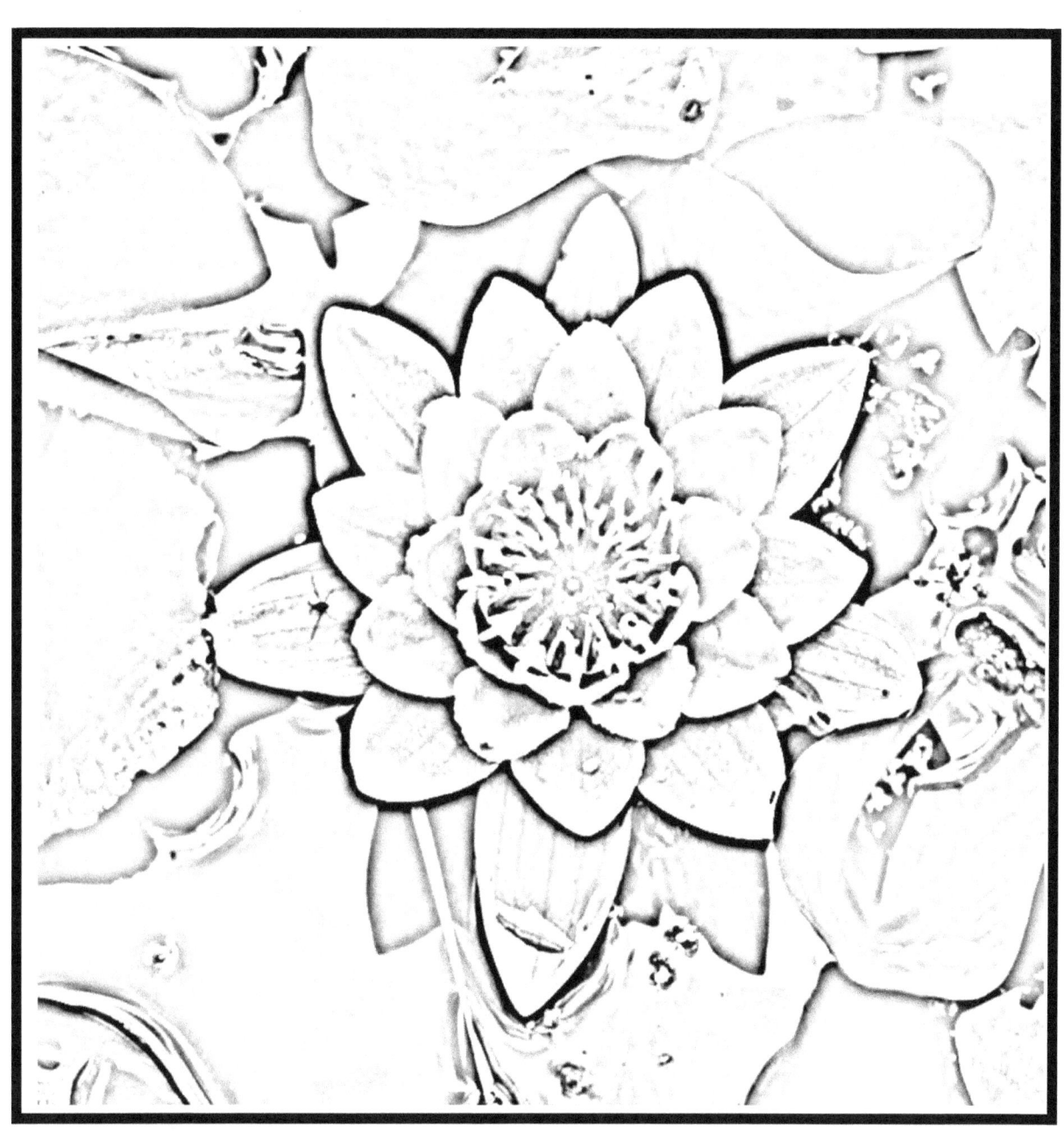

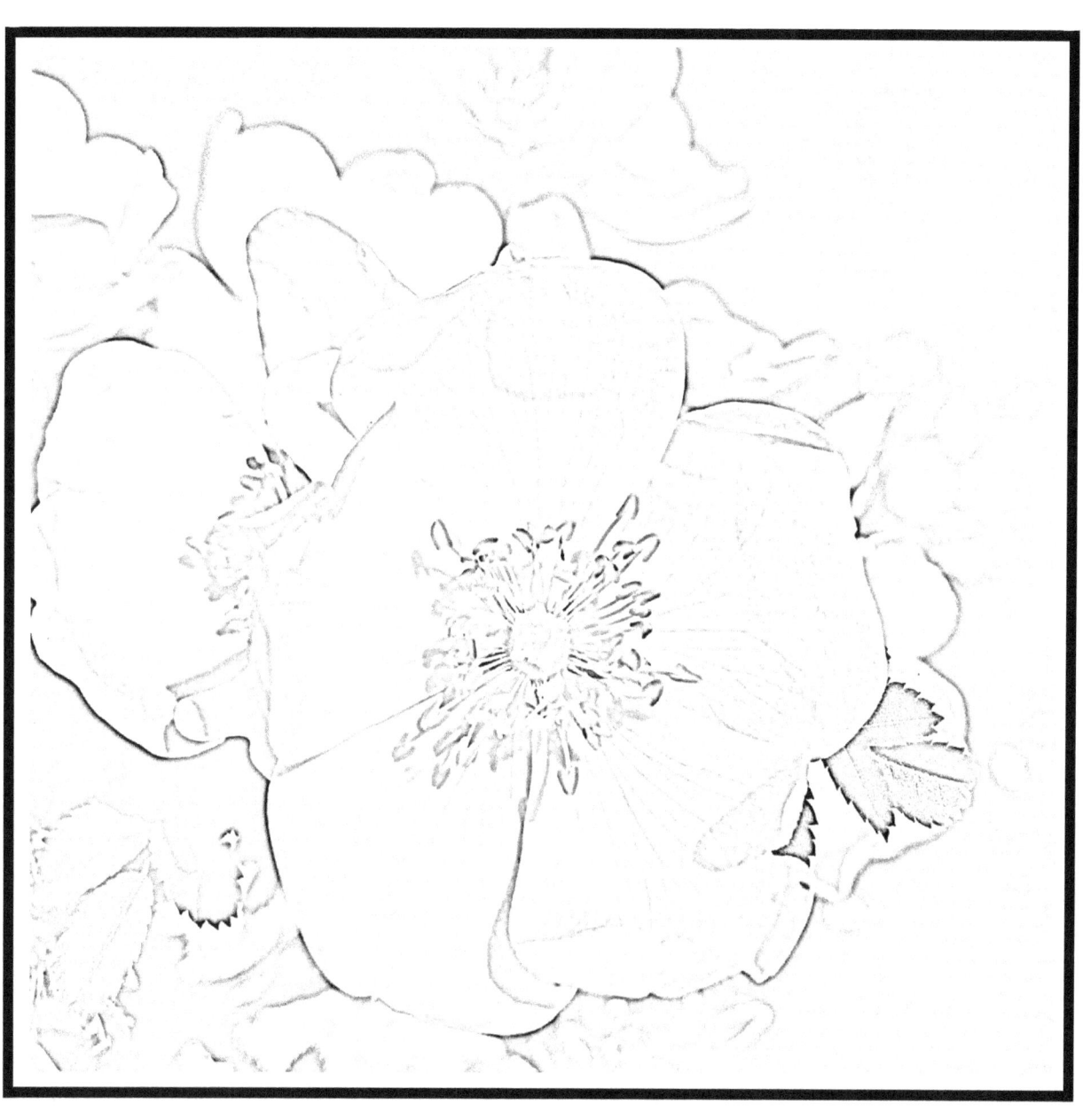

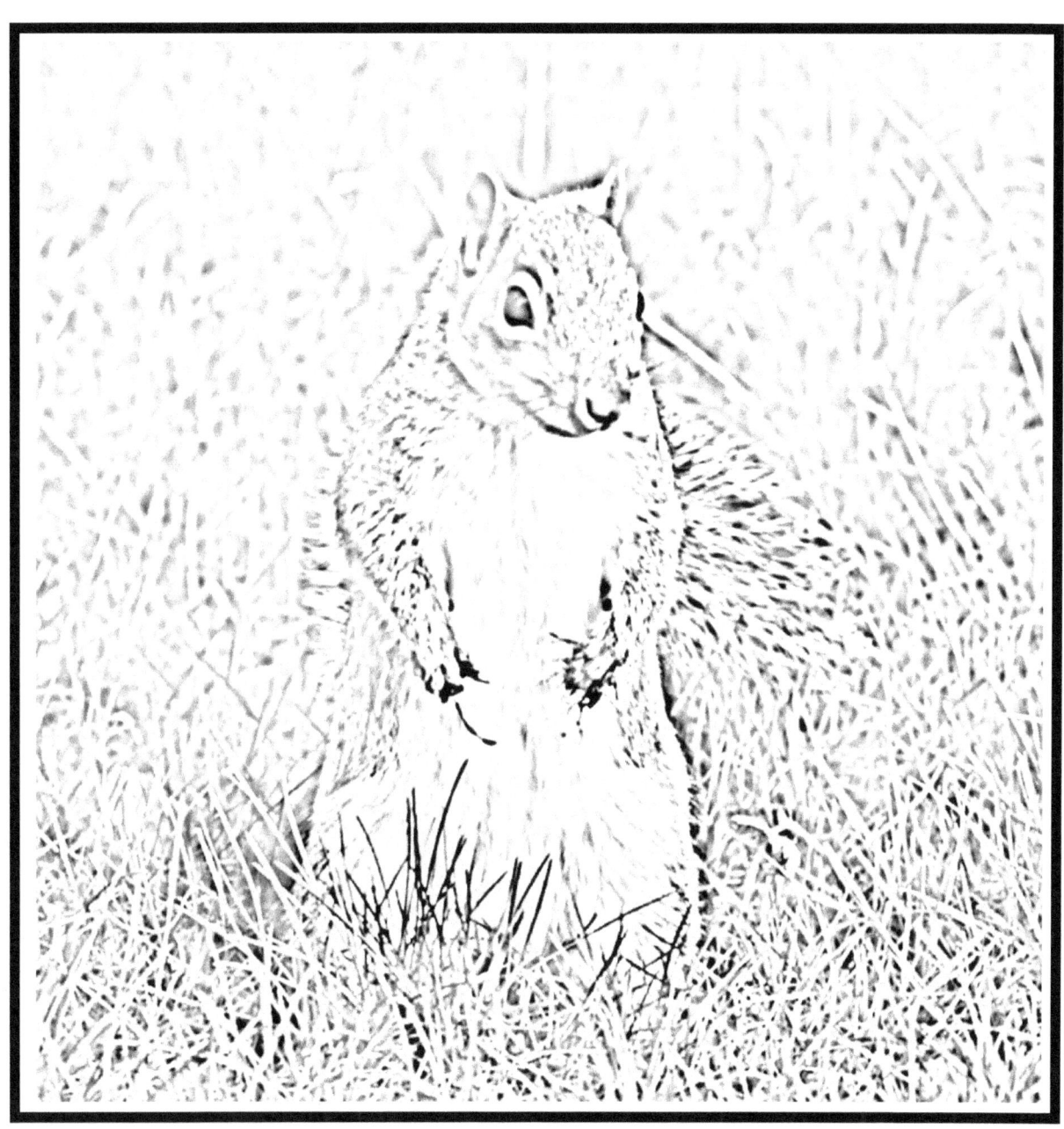

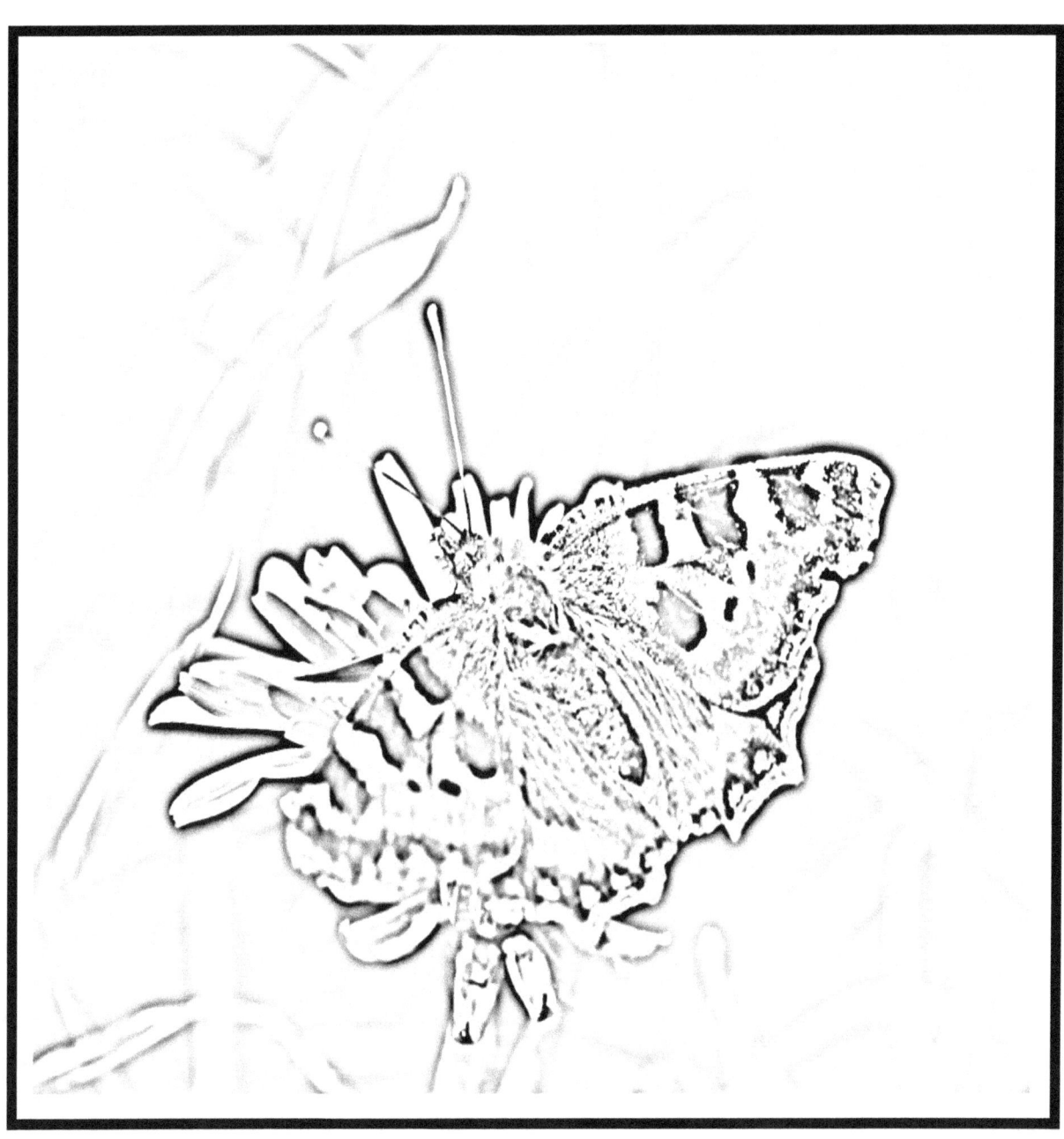

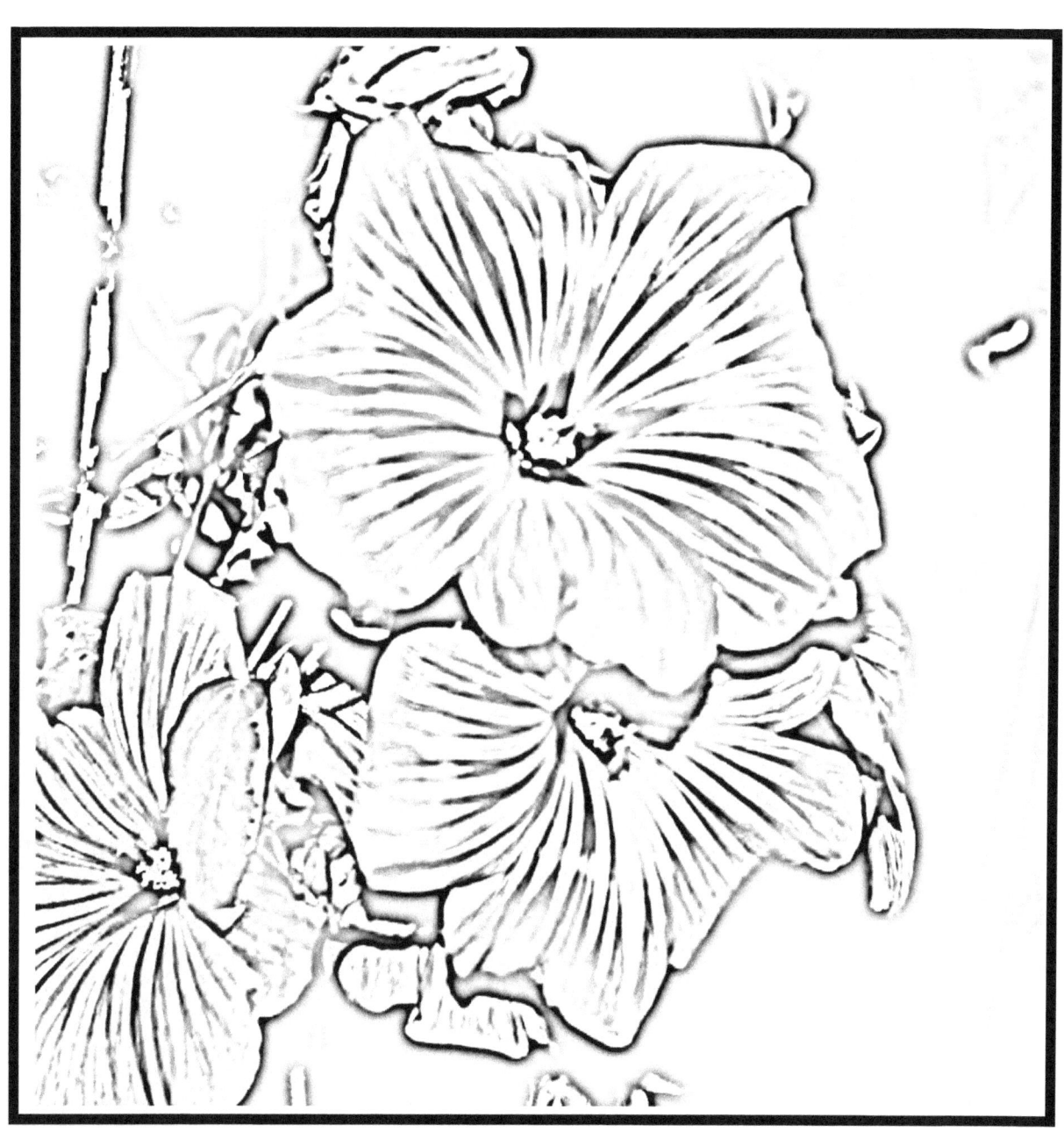

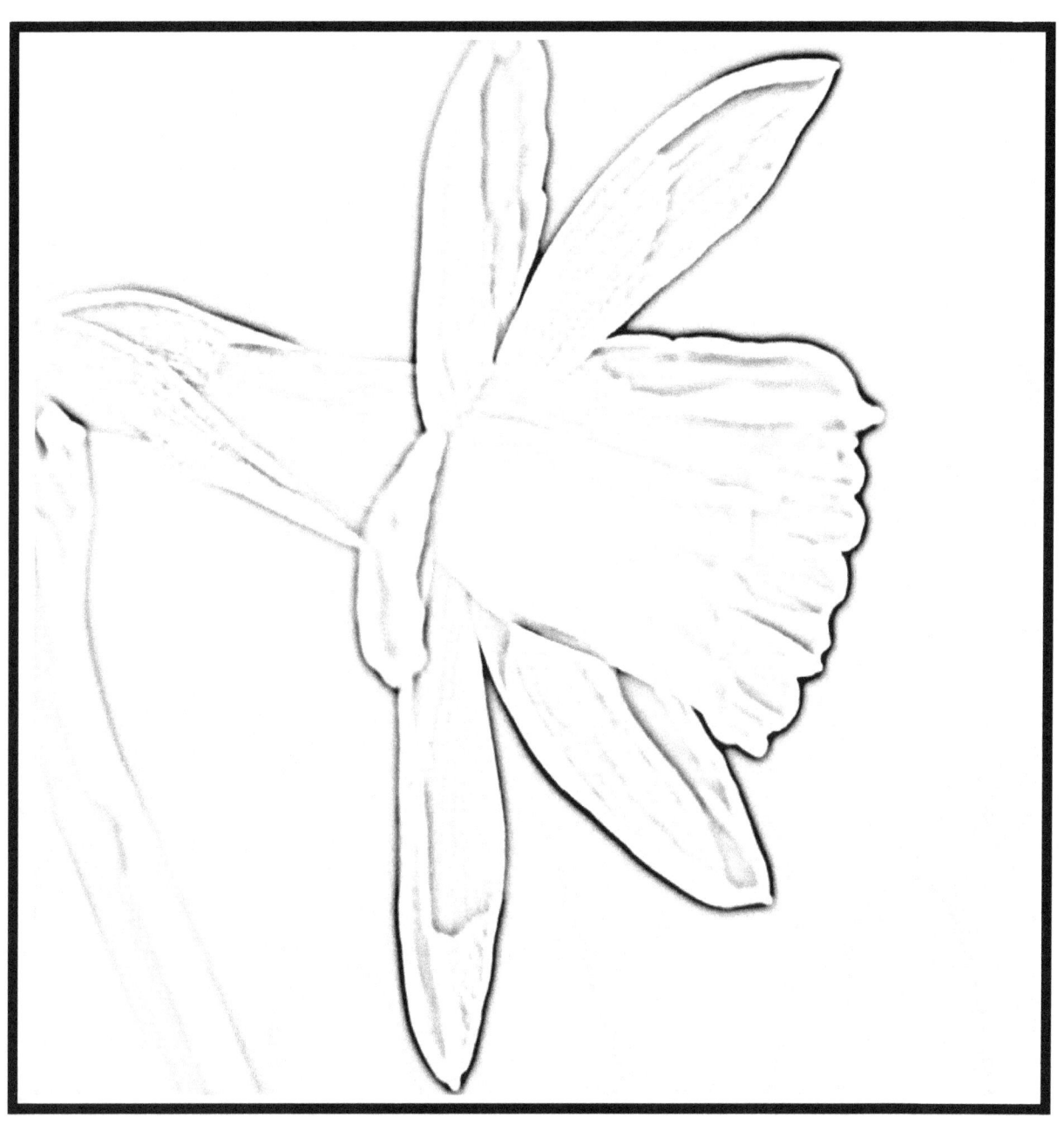

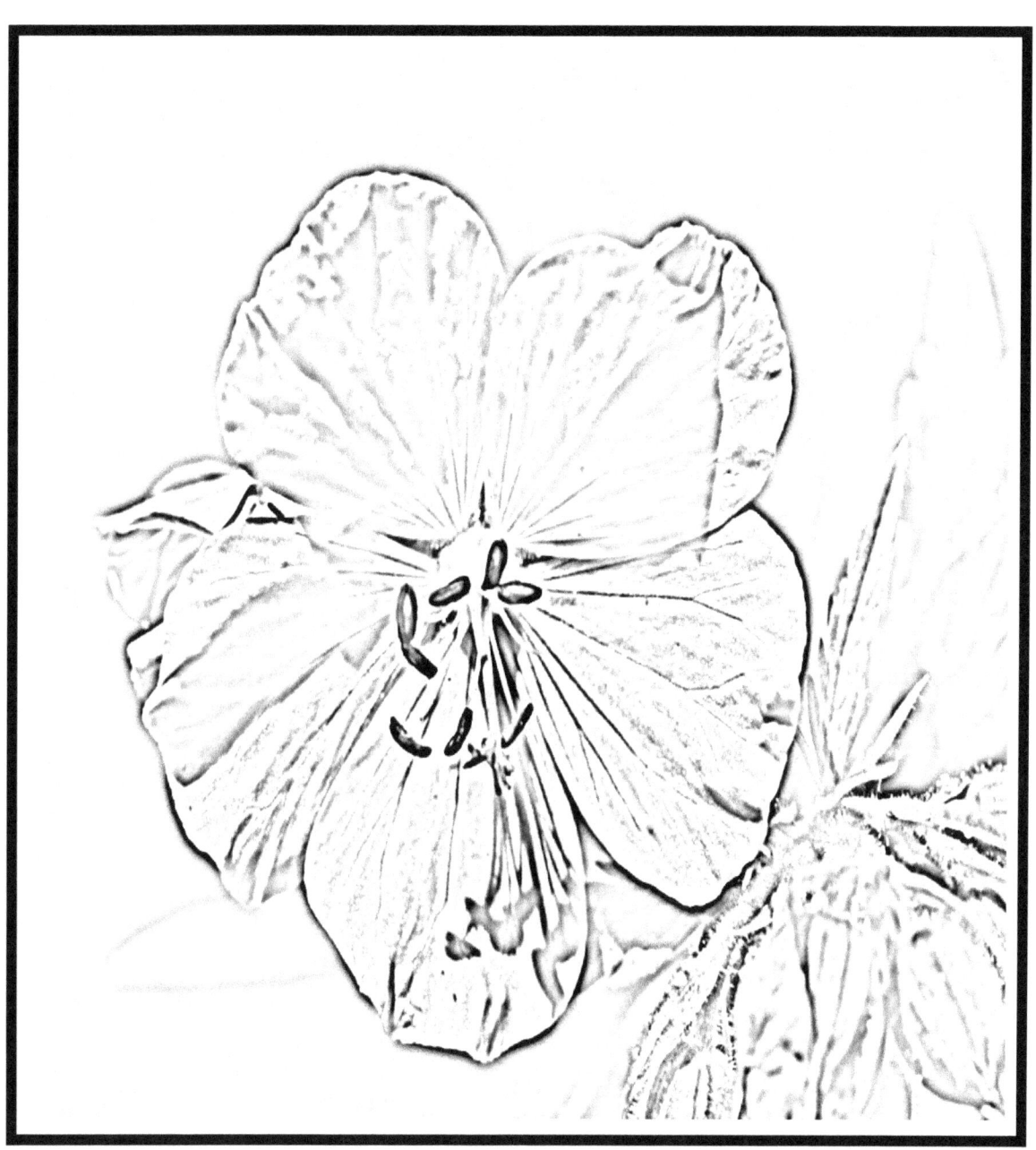

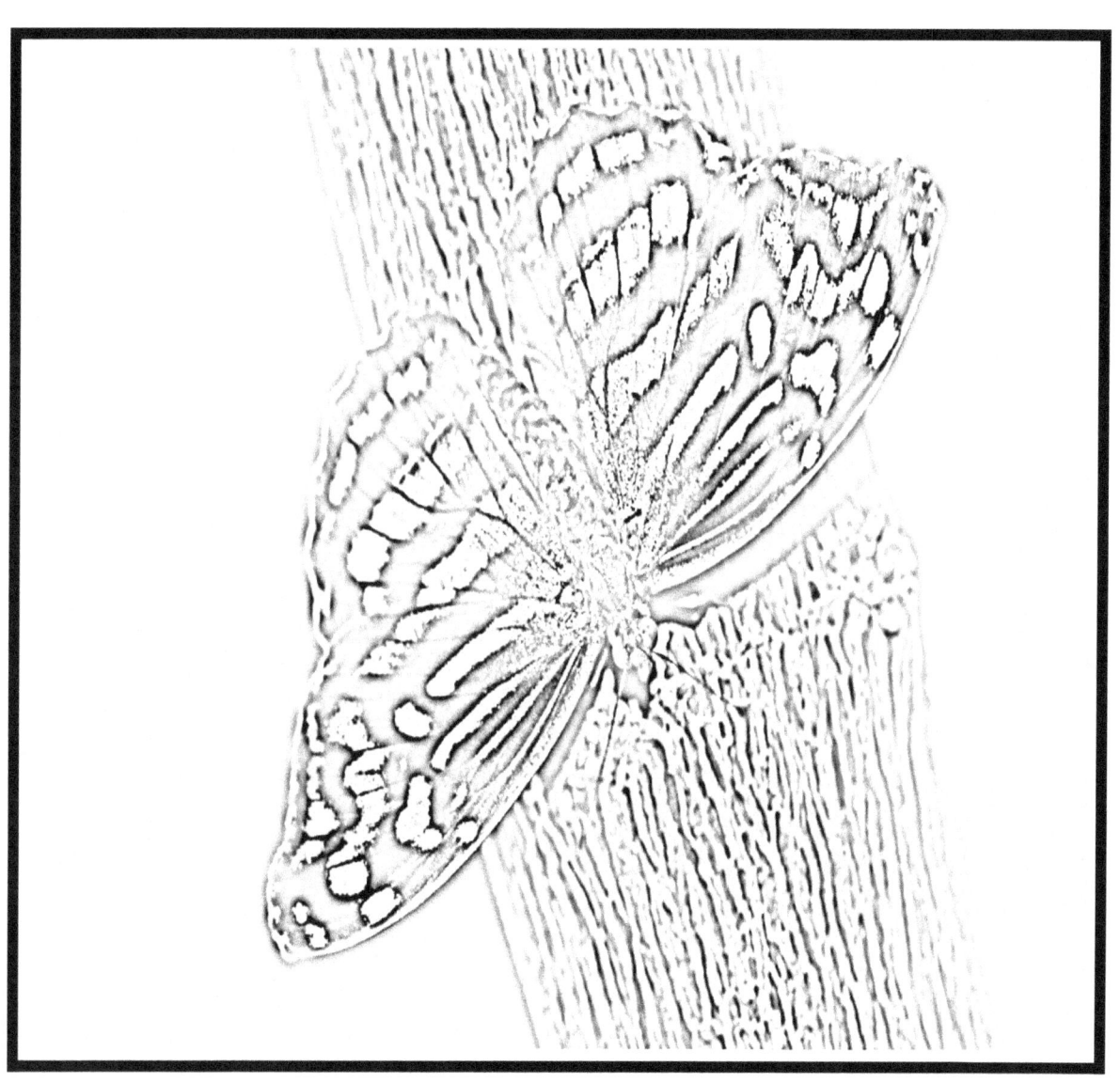

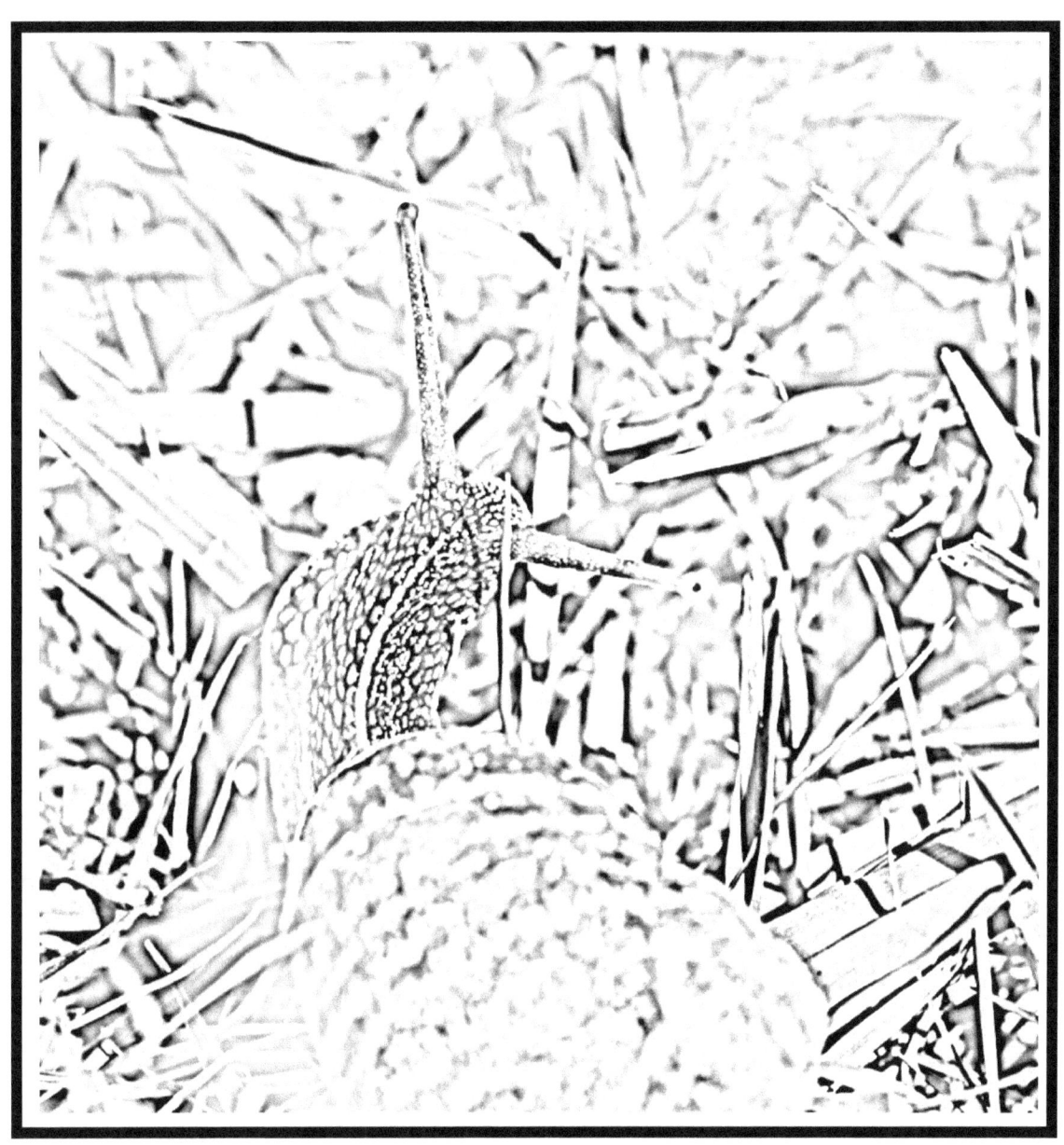

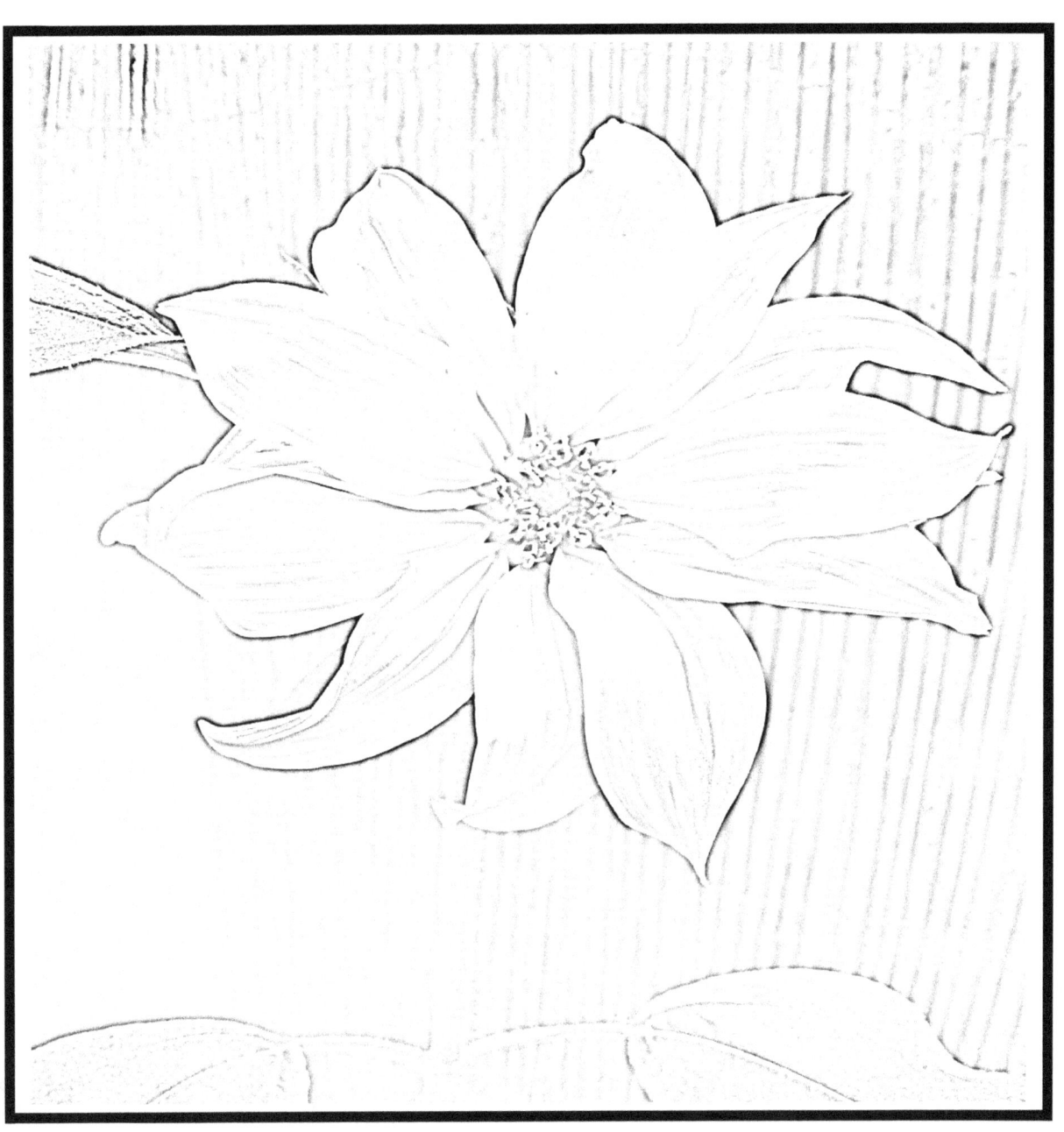

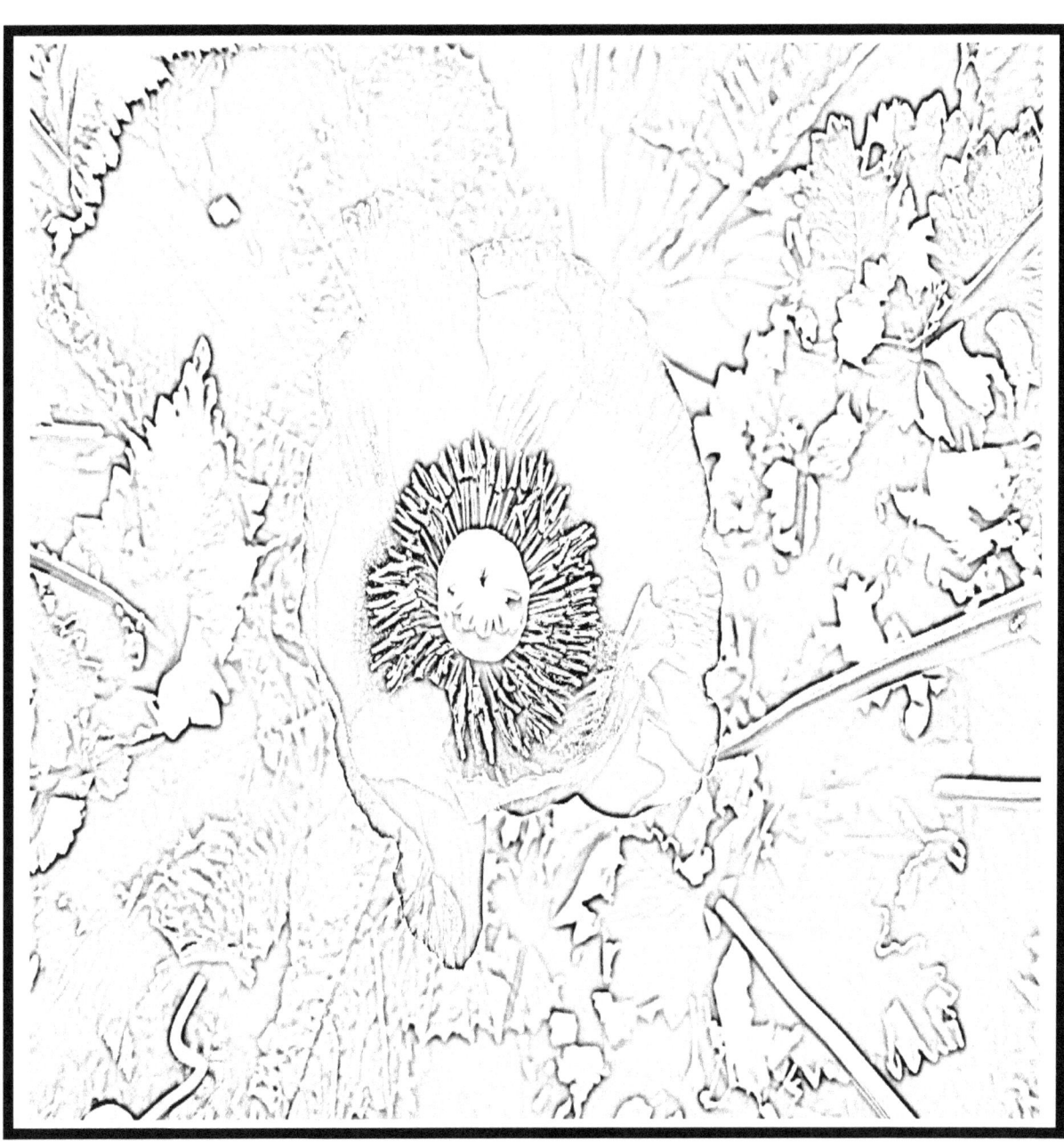

www.ingramcontent.com/pod-product-compliance
Lightning Source LLC
Chambersburg PA
CBHW080550190526
45169CB00007B/2707